The Tangled Web

(An old man's perspective on Life)

Copyright©2018 CWLinton

ISBN: 9781790711994

I remember seeing a magic trick once that initially took my breath away. A man walks into a large gymnasium dressed only in a tee shirt and shorts holding a tray. The tray had a billiard ball underneath a small cloth as he walked towards three people sitting on stools in the centre of the floor. Each in turn was offered to feel under the cloth and confirm that the billiard ball was still there, and once all three had done this he delicately took two fingers and whipped away the cloth ...the billiard ball was gone! We're baffled by many aspects of our world in this way such as finance and politics and as a consequence allow these masters to practice these abstract arts without questioning it. Once I learned that the billiard ball trick was achieved because the third person offered to check was in on the game and had skillfully pocketed the ball it was no longer magic to me. In the same way so many people shy away from 'politics' because they don't know the mechanics of the trick but trust me it is just a trick, or rather an illusion and once you begin to question it you realise how simple the trick is and how we've all been fooled, and most significantly who's benefitting from this.

It's easier to fool people than to convince them
that they have been fooled

Mark Twain

I think progress has always been made by two
flames that burn within the human heart, the
flame of anger against injustice and the flame
of hope that you can build a better world

Tony Benn

Once upon a time there was a ship blown onto the rocks of a distant island thousands of miles from the shipping lanes. Fifty souls survived and all that night and all the next day anyone who was able worked tirelessly swimming back and forth to salvage anything they could, food, clothes, tools before the sea broke it on the reef. Once they'd established themselves on the beach they started to explore their home, not knowing how long they'd be there. There seemed to be an abundance of fresh water, fruit, wildlife to hunt and materials to build a settlement as they began to plan their stay.
One member came up with an idea. "I know, this is what we'll do. We'll choose two burdens out of our group and then pamper them. We'll build them a vast luxurious shelter with as many rooms as our labour will allow and keep it maintained. We'll build a defence around it that no one can enter and we'll hunt, fish and gather tirelessly and give it all to them. If they decide to throw out any scraps of food we'll gratefully accept them and we'll sleep out in the open on the poorest stretch of the beach. Being sick or injured won't be an excuse and they'll just have to suffer or die so that we can continue to pamper our glorious burdens" And they all agreed!
A year later their numbers had dwindled to just over thirty as the burdens became more accustomed to their luxurious lifestyle, and would often talk of how lucky the thirty were to still be alive. The none burdens even had a bucket of fresh water so that they could quench their thirsts sparingly between the back-breaking chores. Life was good. Then one day a cry came from on top of the high hill "Ship ahoy". They all stopped what they were doing and ran down to the beach to see it on the horizon. One shouted "Quickly light the beacon" but as they were running to it the burdens stopped them. "Wait, what are you doing? Haven't we all survived and don't we all have everything we want and need?" They looked around at each other and watched the ship sail away into the distance

CONTENTS

1 Evolution of an Animal

2 Consequences of Evolution

3 Self Delusion

4 The Rigged System

5 Conditioning the Slaves

6 Divide and Rule

7 Executive Action

8 Epilogue

Introduction

The thoughts expressed herein might seem a little disjointed and disconnected, but that's because I've found in life that its problems boil down to a handful of significant issues which in themselves have a wide-ranging history and consequences and so are inextricably intertwined. It may seem like an old man's ramblings, and in essence I guess it is, but everything is connected. A simple truth that resonates with me is that we all have equality of birthright, everything belongs to all of us and the establishment raison d'être is to distract from this. I feel like I'm one of a minority who are passengers on a bus being driven by a crazed driver. Some of us are desperately trying to fight our case to wrest the steering wheel from him while the others are laughing, seemingly unawares as they simply tell us to sit nearer the back if we're so worried! If you sat any group of people down and discussed what was morally right and proper for the world everyone would agree on everything ..so why do people vote differently? Life conditions you to accept so many things, after all it's easier to try and assimilate into the system than it is to fight it. There comes a time however when you have to look at the big picture, which incidentally you're part of, and ask basic questions like "Should I have had my life determined by whether my parents were of modest income or left a more privileged legacy for me?" After all you aren't your parent's possession any more than they're yours, so why do some people get a head start and then stay there because of it? How did the person driving their grand car, sending their children to university and taking two holidays a year get all that while we're scraping a living? What great gift do they bring to society to make them so deserving of their vastly more privileged share compared to us, and are they justified in accusing us of not working as hard as them or not being as gifted? Is it a coincidence that the people with those benefits want to conserve that system? Why are we conditioned to accept that this strata of society are the executors of this planet and we're simply guests to be accommodated within it? It's like the Emperor's new clothes, where most of us have no idea why these cathedrals of administration all around us that employ these people are there or what their purpose is, but everyone else seems to know so we just won't say anything and trust they'll keep 'our' society ticking over. Most of us end up in a life of constant worry over which job we'll get, then if we'll get a promotion, and then at the end we worry about whether we'll have enough pension to survive as we live out our last days reflecting on how we could've done better. Thomas Jefferson once wrote "We hold these truths to be self-evident: that all men are created equal; that they are endowed by their Creator with certain unalienable rights; that among these are life, liberty, and the pursuit of happiness". These great sentiments embody how society should be run, but these ideals have never been actively pursued, least of all in their country of origin. The reason why nothing changes is because the things you're willing to accept lessen as you grow older, but by the time you're not prepared to accept these injustices at all you've passed the point where you're prepared to rebel. Whereas individual failings of social structures may be discussed at length, rarely is the issue of a common origin of this universal failing ever even offered. I hope to point out that there is a common origin to all of this, and furthermore that any debate about it is deliberately concealed so that the truth we're deluded into believing is an illusion and that we only need to think about it a little to realise its truth. It's like looking at a drawing that's an optical Illusion, where at first it seems to look like the profile of an attractive woman, but once your eyes acclimatise to the contour lines you suddenly see a gnarled old woman's face in a head scarf.

We live in a time where fear and hatred of groups and individuals dominate the social and political agendas, an environment which seems to be a trend playing itself out like a cancer re-infecting society every few decades. Separate from this occasional resurgence however is a world which never seems to change. Ask yourself whether you think a just world should allow a mother to be dragged from her home in a glare of publicity and her possessions thrown onto the street by a baying crowd, or children beaten by soldiers. Is it acceptable that a girl born in the Third World is mutilated and enslaved to the whim of the male sections of her community? Should a single mother be left to fend for herself and her children? Should a woman be so desperate for survival that she sells her body and is then arrested for it? Is it fair that the vast majority of the world's population and their descendants will never rise above poverty level and so seek escape from its grim reality in a descending cycle of drug abuse? Why should any individual have access to millions or billions yet parents of sick children have to beg for charity? How is it these injustices are enshrined in the laws of this world and are allowed to go, not only uncorrected, but also deliberately ignored or even encouraged to the extent of war? Is it that the resources of the planet are so limited that we find ourselves fighting for them in every nook and cranny, or is it all happening in a world where a small elite reap all the rewards of our combined efforts? How has this come about? I've never read any social philosophy, but it's become apparent to me how this structure has developed over time to a broken society designed to benefit a small minority at the expense of the majority and is setting us on a path to Armageddon. These questions and many more have bounced around inside my head for most of my life, and as I approach the end of this journey they shout so loudly I realise just how much I've stifled them and how everyone else does the same. From our earliest days we're led into a belief that the factories, apartments, shops, buses, media the entire infrastructure is a gift provided by benefactors, automatically elevating those providing and administering the system to a higher priority. We forget that we're all born into this life as an equal and instead automatically give these strata an automatic birthright.

The System

Let's look at the structure of any society in as basic a way as we can to understand the mechanics of where the wealth comes from and how it's allocated. When life was simpler we had a barter system, and so whenever we made a transaction we could immediately determine what we were getting as recompense. We could build someone a shelter for their home and decide on getting a pig in return, or if we gave someone a lift to market they could give us some vegetables as our trade. As life becomes more complicated then obviously this system doesn't work, so our 'effort' has to be translated into credit to be used at a later date. Think about that – all of our daily effort, each and every one of us. So as you're heading out for your bus or driving home, while you're answering the telephone, laying a brick or seeing clients, each five minutes of that often stressful and tiring day a little lead pellet drops into a central factory as a token of your state credit contribution along with everyone else's, each one representing a hard earned five minutes of your labour. At the end of the week when you go to collect your share of pellets a spoon and a pair of tweezers are used to meticulously measure your share into a small tin. As you leave you're stopped by a guard who takes out about a third of them and takes them back to the factory to add to the mountain of pellets. While you're walking away you notice someone driving up to the factory through a restricted back door in a beautiful new car, wearing expensive clothes with a large bucket and being saluted by the guards. It would take the contributions of the whole vast crowd of people who've just visited the factory with you and more to fill his bucket for his share. What can this person possibly have done, which great skill must they possess to receive such a vast share of all our contributions as their reward? As you watch him drive back through the gates the guards stop him and take out a small spoon's worth of pellets from his bucket. A man steps out of the big car and starts arguing with the head guard on the rich man's behalf, and after a couple of minutes the guard pours back the spoonful of pellets into the bucket and salutes him as he drives off. You also notice some of those same guards accompanied you to the factory for their tiny share too. On exiting the security gate you're stopped by a distraught looking woman who shakes a tin at you begging for one or two pellets for the medicine for her child as the flashy car toots its horn and the woman has to quickly step back to avoid being knocked over by it.

This might seem an overly dramatic analogy, but trust me it isn't. Throughout our life we're actively encouraged to try and accumulate more than our fair share with the ethic of 'greed is good' being the soundtrack to our life. Look at any commercial on TV, radio or any other media and analyse the message being broadcast out at you. It goes – take as much as you can and we can help you to achieve it, but don't think about who you're taking it from. They must be vigilant in promoting the delusion that wealth is somehow plucked from nowhere like a fruit to be harvested from a faraway island rather than a share to be allocated. There's a finite pool of credit to share and the fact is that if it isn't allocated fairly then in order for anyone to gain someone has to lose. This is the stark reality of our society, where from the time we're born we're automatically relegated to a lower position without even asking ourselves why. As adults large numbers will still allow themselves to accept this bizarre privilege landscape, and see any small crumbs passed their way as a benevolent gift. This simple model illustrates how any society is constructed, your contribution to it and the way those contributions are ultimately allocated. In reality there are people who own the entire factory and its pellets and the situation is getting worse. It would soften the blow if someone getting a bucketful of credit was a great thinker, an engineer or artist, but knowing that these people are simply the unimaginative manipulators within our society being allowed to rape and pillage our hard earned labour quite frankly makes my blood boil ...and it should make yours boil too! Let's remind ourselves of those wise words: "We hold these truths to be self-evident: that all men are created equal; that they are endowed by their Creator with certain unalienable rights; that among these are life, liberty, and the pursuit of happiness". We have to ask ourselves how we can fix it, and to understand fully we need to know how it came to be like this in the first place.

1 EVOLUTION OF AN ANIMAL

Three Urges

We are just an animal! Whatever your religious or academic beliefs this truth has to be recognised as factual evidence, and that any actions we take or decisions we make are a direct consequence of this fact. Anyone who has delusions of a Divine hand creating us simply has to look at a collection of skeletons from lizards all the way through to mammals and if you truly think we're anything but another species developed through evolution then you're deluding yourself. We certainly are a unique species, and take notice I didn't say special, in as much as the development of our brain has become the major contributory factor in our evolution. Nature has experimented with developing various aspects of each organism's morphology over the staggeringly immense timescales of our world from the humble bacteria to the largest beasts, where some have developed larger muscles, grown or shrunk in size, developed wings or the ability to fly or return to the water, but prior to our species any accelerated brain development had simply been to accommodate these structural developments. Nature favours species that can adapt, and whereas a creature that had evolved to lose its fur would die if the climate suddenly cooled, an animal that could work out it can take another beast's fur would survive. So it is that our ability to adapt has seen us become the most dominant adaptive species the planet has ever seen, and that perceptiveness has brought us to this unequalled dominance we have today, and it also brings consequences. We weren't 'designed' we weren't 'put' here, we're simply a consequence of the Universe, but human nature won't allow this reality to exist in our consciousness and so we construct reasons for existence and purposes. In some ways it's an endearing quality, but the more influence we have over this tiny island paradise in the vastness of space the more we need to listen to the voices of educated men and women and not the instinctive voice of that beast within. Up until very recently in geological terms every species whether an insect, lizard or mammal that had ever lived followed the same linear programme, where each day was a struggle to survive and reproduce and nature honed this programme along that linear path. Our species was no different, and in fact my argument is that these traits are so engrained in our fabric that we're still no different, but our ability to influence the world and extend our control now threatens not just us but also other species and the planet itself because of our inability or refusal to recognise that we are just another animal. We are the same as all other species, in that we're all guided by the same two characteristics programmed into us by evolution, namely the survival urge and the legacy urge. Survival is maybe the simplest trait to understand and really doesn't need any explanation, the legacy urge however is a little more abstract. We could contrast the same example in two different circumstances to understand in very graphic terms what's meant by this. Imagine that one day you're out with the other hunters and a bear comes charging out at your group. Now you may have bonds to a certain degree with them, but as an old saying goes – you don't need to be able to run faster than the bear you just have to be able to run faster than the people you're with! Granted you may contribute to a defence of them, but if circumstances overwhelm you the survival instinct would make you choose the more grim solution. Now imagine that another time you're out one day with your family when the bear charges, would you adopt the same attitude? This conundrum puzzled naturalists and other evolutionary philosophers as it seemed to be in direct conflict with the survival protocol. Why would we defend our direct descendants at the cost of severe injury or even death? Remember that this urge to defend your offspring or other family members isn't uniquely human, far from it, it's part of every species that has ever lived. So how can this be explained? Well it's quite simple, nature has tailored us to follow this principle so that we can pass on our genes. It isn't just about individual survival but rather an ever evolving imperative honed by nature in order that the dominant survivor we've become lives on genetically. Even though we don't make a conscious decision to lay down our life, just as with the survival urge we have no control over it, it controls us. Any species that evolved the ability to rationalise and consider their destiny would, as a consequence utilise that ability to reinforce those two subconscious fundamental principles to its own benefit, it just so happened that around 200,000 years ago that species was us.

A turning point was around 40,000 years ago and marked a boundary between us as just another beast in the game of survival to a more sentient creature, the hunter-gatherer would become a farmer. If we put ourselves in the position of our ancestors at the dawn of that new era we can identify with them at that basic level. If you came across a bush laden with succulent, nutrient rich fruit would you gorge yourself as much as you could or would you store it for you and your family to eat later? When we reach a point where our store of food, clothes and other possessions grows ever larger not only do we still want to keep them for ourselves but our legacy urge means we'll use our wits to pass on these advantages to our family. If we compare this with a more complex, larger society when does common sense become greed? The game has quite suddenly changed from mere survival to a creature with the ability to try and outwit other members of their species to control these two pre-programmed selfish urges. If we look around us at the natural world we see behaviours that have been part of every species since life began, where posturing, fighting, tactical manoeuvring involves climbing the ladder of dominance or trying to assimilate into this life or death struggle. Our ascendancy from the shackles that all these other species have been chained to for over four billion years is seen as the accepted emancipation from this struggle, and finally without the necessity to survive we can enjoy the fruits of our privileged evolution. Unfortunately certain elements within our species haven't evolved beyond this basic evolutionary level, and instead of enjoying a communal life for the good of all mankind we are still dominated by these manipulators. In the modern world, these people don't have the limitations of acquiring a few fields, their greed urge never stops and so you have a situation where one individual 'acquires' a wealth that's a billion fold more than the average citizen and dominance over vast international areas. We may have taken the man away from hunter-gathering but we haven't taken the hunter-gatherer out of the man! A higher cognitive ability however has given us a dangerous tool with which to further outwit our fellow homo sapiens.

The Tribal Urge

If we think of another predator like a lion for instance, hunting a wildebeest on the plains, the lion won't take on too big a beast or too big a group in case of injury. Similarly if a rival predator challenged the lion it would have a pre-programmed instinct to choose whether or not discretion was the better part of valour, or to put it simply it would have an unconscious protocol for fight or flight. Now the lion hasn't 'considered' this it's simply following instinct, it hasn't rationalised the consequences, a human on the other hand has this ability and is aware of its own mortality. Can you imagine the first animal to have the awareness each day that, not only could they suffer serious injury or lose their family but also that one of these days will be their last. Since the dawn of life nature had adapted the characteristics necessary for the survival and furtherance of each species, and four and a half billion years later we have the first instance of 'contrived evolution' the Tribal imperative. How many of us today from our relatively safe environments could comfortably walk practically naked into a hostile world dominated by savage predators and other groups of opposing hunter-gatherers to risk injury or death in order to feed and protect our family? It's easy to imagine the irresistible appeal of a belief, reinforced by other tribe members, that a mystical tribal leader or group of elders is somehow looking after your welfare, so that even if disaster befalls you the worst that can happen is you'll join their elevated council of elders. This would have the effect that not only would you accept danger more easily, but that death may even be the gateway to a greater, more wonderful existence where pain and suffering have no meaning. So the beast that once had an inexplicable urge to pass on their legacy in a subconscious way now has a belief that their 'spirit' will also live on, giving rise to ancestor myths across the entire scope of our species' development. This coping mechanism is a collaborative device which served our ancestors for eons, and is almost as firmly programmed into us as the survival urge and its related legacy urge. This contrived protocol has not only outlived its usefulness, but has now become a reinforcement of the two selfish urges into a powerful instinct that has not only allowed rampant corruption but also threatens our extinction.

It tugs at our imagination to contemplate the slow dawning of the realities of these primitive humans as they became more aware of their surroundings. Stone tools have been discovered that are millions of years old and pre date even our homo species, but around 40,000 years ago the first known cave paintings appeared and mark a boundary between that hunter-gatherer and the more sentient being they were becoming as they began to control agriculture and farming. It would've been accompanied by the development of music and a curiosity about the mysteries of nature, in other words Art and Science. This fascination of comparing and wondering at the differences between the animal we were in those dark times and the animal we were becoming and the natural world around us, regardless of the personal benefits to ourselves, is the mark of civilization. So Art and Science become an end in themselves, pure fascination and wonderment invested in us as a consequence of our evolutionary heritage for no other reason than we have the capacity to contemplate them. Philosophy weighs up the 'evils' inherent from our dark past against the aspiration of making a better world, where logic has little meaning, but a deep instinct about what's civilized and compassionate tugs at what we feel is 'right'. The Brothers Grimm documented many stories that pique the imagination, and their attraction is this comparison between a distant world that exists in the dark recesses of our imagination, and the subjects of paintings cause us to contemplate many uncomfortable or thought-provoking scenarios. This is the crux of how our species has separated and developed into the contemporary model we have today – those who largely remain the beast with their single-minded selfish aims and those who largely choose compassion and wonderment. If we picture Mafia figures taking Caravaggio's Nativity from the Oratory of San Lorenzo in the middle of the night for nefarious selfist reasons, or Isis extremists destroying ancient sculptures at Palmyra for some twisted tribalist doctrine, then this highlights perfectly the contrast between the beast and the enlightened human. The beasts will forever embrace the selfish, instinctive imperatives of nature and the dreamers will consider the consequences. Ask yourself if challenged to describe which you were, who would want to ally themselves with the beast? On the other hand I think we'd all like to be considered dreamers, yet a large proportion of civilization choose to remain the beast without recognising that fact, and this is the root of the historic social misery and possible annihilation we face today. Throughout recorded history the most insidious device used among us is the active manipulation of this Tribal urge by other members of society, an instinct that served us well during the dark days of the beast, but it has no place in a post hunter-gatherer society. A supernatural deity or deities may have been an extremely useful comfort blanket to ancient peoples surviving in a ruthless world, but that delusion is completely redundant today other than in the field of the arts and its divisive consequences are the seeds of misery.

Tribalism in Action

 If we consider the way societies have evolved the original model of oppression is as simple as you can imagine. Basically an individual or individuals highly motivated by the legacy and greed principles would subjugate their local population to bend them to their will. If there were strategic difficulties they could threaten to kill people close to them or destroy or seize their properties, but that was still just a subtle variation on the theme. The model has never changed in thousands of years, but as societies have grown and information technology has advanced the perpetrators have had to refine their techniques, and this is where the Tribal urge has been exploited over the last few thousand years. Just as a lion will exercise caution when faced with a threatening adversary so these Mafia style gangs have employed the Tribal urge to stabilise their control and supplement their armoury. The people being oppressed would've been aware on a subconscious level that there really wasn't much they could do about the situation without great personal risk anyway from these aggressive manipulators, and so this coping strategy is in large part collaborative, an acceptance of the inevitable. These bad shepherds will also come to believe that in some way they're special, when they look around and see the vast majority of society scraping a living while they live a luxurious, privileged lifestyle. Many even come to believe that they're 'chosen', how else could their exalted position be explained? They believe in a very real sense that the rest of us are simple children who have to be subdued in order to allow them to run societies, and as such they see their responsibility as keeping us repressed so as not to impede their control. The popular story of King Canute may or may not be true, but it's fully believable that this delusion of having Divine control over the world would extend to a monarch believing that he could command the tides not to come in. They're assisted in their Divine narcissism by various members of the suppressed factions who treat naivety almost as a virtue! These sections of society, being confused by the mechanics in operation about them, reinforce their shared ignorance as a bonding tool, where a shared subservience comforts them and negates the necessity for decision making. Consequently we find history littered with Kings, Emperors and Caesars who acted in the name of various deities and leave statues and civic monuments as a reinforcement and reminder to history of their immortality and legacy. The success of this acquiescence by the suppressed peoples to a bizarre ideal of the world is evident in for example the Richard III Society, where people will argue over whether he was a 'good' or a 'bad' King. Some people are easily susceptible to an idealised version of reality where characters are stylized into simply being good or evil to describe a fairy tale where they've created a world of order, chivalry and decency and it illustrates the ease with which these historical barbarians were allowed to hone their craft. The danger is that although many people see this deception for what it was, they labour under the misapprehension that this system is a thing of the past when this is far from the truth.

2 CONSEQUENCES OF EVOLUTION

Divide and Rule

In order for the greed elite to control us more manageably they have to stop us organising and focus our support towards them, and so they divide us by using that prehistoric trigger which they've learned can easily be activated, especially amongst those of lesser intellect or low income who crave an instant explanation for and solution to their predicament. Tribalism manifests itself in many ways, bigotry, racism, patriotism, religion and nationalism, they're just sanitised titles to justify Tribalism. It doesn't require the believer to rationalise or use compassion, there's no need for logic or empathy because it's simply our birthright ...isn't it? Anyone reading that sentence who doesn't realise how barbaric that is is in danger of identifying with the perpetrators of the Holocaust and other ethnic cleansing atrocities. In order for manipulators to use your Tribalism trigger effectively they must first de-humanise the targets, and they do this with your collusion. Anyone who doesn't have empathy for another distressed human being either has some form of psychopathic pathology or has allowed that prehistoric Tribalist trigger to be activated. Taking the selfism urge into consideration let's imagine two different scenarios. Firstly you're asked by unscrupulous individuals to act as a look-out while they commit a jewellery robbery. Imagine that you know that you'll never be linked to the crime whatever the outcome, and you'll receive £5000 for your part. Now imagine you've been offered the same reward to stand by while a small child is brutally beaten by an adult. Whether it be Bosnia or Bavaria, ordinary men and women can be led to see other human beings as none human if they let their defences fall prey to malevolent manipulators, particularly if they're disassociated from the acts themselves. Atrocities aren't perpetrated because of unfeeling, hate-filled individuals, these people will exist in our societies whatever the contemporary circumstances. No they're committed because disinterested people look the other way or even assist them. We're not simple hunter-gatherers anymore we're in transition, where forensic, logical science is tempered with compassion. We don't recognise folklore and fairy tales any longer unless it's within the realm of art and literature, and it should be accepted that compassion is a trait we should all try to encompass and aspire to. So to what degree is that Tribalism urge your personal guide? There's a marvellous sketch in Dick Clement and Ian La Frenais' "Whatever happened to The Likely Lads?" where one character Terry awkwardly tries to justify his hatred or mistrust of ethnic groups and nationalities to his friend Bob, and if you haven't seen it check it out. How 'Terry Collier' are you? Do you genuinely believe that being English, Scottish, German, American or whatever makes you different? Special? Selected? Do you accept easily the advice and opinions of your peers without personally considering the validity of the issues yourself? Do you find that you 'want' to agree with them? Well let's forget bestial, prehistoric instincts and consider the science behind your argument then.

Scientific Evidence

Should we form a conclusion and then look for corroborative evidence to support it, excluding all others, or should we analyse the evidence and only then come to a conclusion? When we think of geological timescales with reference to anatomical changes within species we talk in terms of millions or even billions of years. Each species diversifies, so for instance we can see that a zebra and a horse are related as are lions and tigers. The same was true for our 'hominid' species, and as far as we know the last known related members Neanderthals along with Homo Floresiensis and Denisovans disappeared as recently as around 50,000 to 40,000 years ago, but as of today we are the last surviving species of hominid on Earth. Think about that, not Caucasian, Negroid or Mongoloid, not Russian, African or French but one unique species, this isn't supposition or speculation it's forensic fact. The study of DNA heritage, although incomplete in certain aspects, has shown the truth of our species' lineage historically, and what it tells us is that we may have different physical characteristics but we are one race, one species, one tribe if you like. For anyone under the delusion that for instance peoples with African features are somehow inferior, consider this. We're all a hybrid hominid, with the general consensus being that Neanderthals were less sophisticated technologically and artistically. When our species migrated out of Africa into Europe we interbred, and so the more European you are the higher level of Neanderthal DNA, and the more African you are the more likelihood you'll have none and therefore be a more pure race of Homo sapiens! So where does this leave white supremacist's doctrine of superiority? DNA profiling can describe physical characteristics, but there never has been an engineer's gene, an artist's gene or a doctor's gene. Tribal differences are simply contrived ones, so if you defend your tribal 'rights' in preference to a farmer from New Delhi, a driver from Moscow or a factory worker from Angola then you're simply embracing this fallacy for the benefit to you personally using tribalist justification by proxy through your manipulators. Don't forget these same targets will be being manipulated by their Tribalists too, using your hostility towards them as their justification. Anyone who continues to insist that members of our species are inferior or superior because of the way they look or where they were born are simply embracing and embellishing a lie and failing to recognise that the only differences are perceived and manufactured through Tribalism. These are facts not opinions or theories, and the only debate is whether or not you choose to deliberately ignore them and pretend it isn't true for your own selfish ends at the cost of the rest of your wider society in your pursuit of selfism. Extreme right wing agitators will try to appeal to a simple message in people, and keeping it simple is the key to understanding the issues. The difference is that these Tribalists use the pseudo logic of prehistoric instincts as their baseline instead of rational morality and compassion. There is no right or wrong attitude from a scientific standpoint, it's simply whether you'd like to see the world as compassionate or competitive. Devious conservative politicians have learned that using rampant tribalism would bring their reign to an end just as much as allowing people to see the compassionate truth of simplicity would, so they tread a careful minefield of deception in-between.

Lions led by Donkeys
We have allowed our world to become dominated by people who essentially have no skills to contribute to society but are simply devious manipulators. Imagine you were shipwrecked on a desert island and you'd

established the basics like fresh water, food and shelter and now you can devote yourselves to the maintenance of your community and leisure time. The majority of you will work your share, some of you will come up with innovate engineering ideas, some may have ways of entertaining you or making your environment more attractive to live in with artistic decoration. If you have no particular skill it doesn't matter, we can all contribute in some way whether it's fetching and carrying or providing muscle for engineering projects etc. Eventually you'll each grow old but it's hardly an extra effort to support the aged, and their gift they give is their life experience and wisdom to the children and adults alike. Now I said most people would do their share, but what about the others? Among the none-skilled people some will feign injury or sickness to avoid doing their share, and once they realise they can get away with it without too much of a challenge they'll play that card relentlessly in order to gain a lesser input to the community. Also among this section looking to acquire more than their fair share are people who whisper behind people's backs, telling various members of the group that a particular person has said something about them, probably telling the same thing to that other person too in a deliberate effort to create distrust. These manipulators may have difficulty in dividing people on rational grounds, so they see that a minority of the members of your community are bald. This provides them with an ideal tool to demote this section to the benefit of 'the rest of us' because of the undeniable visual evidence. Even though we'd gotten on perfectly well before with these bald people and hadn't even noticed their baldness, now we 'realise' through our confidant that we just hadn't seen it until now and allow our prehistoric tribal instinct to be triggered. Eventually these manipulators achieve their aim by becoming a confidant and a rallying point as they gather a group around them as a trusted source, slowly dividing the community up into dissatisfied factions. This story has played itself out countless times and is the source of every political intrigue and war in human history. Historians, political journalists and researchers show an almost sycophantic glee at characters whether fictitious or actual, be it Robert Cecil or Gatsby where these ambitious, callous figures play out their destructive games using Tribalist delusions to torture, kill and cause untold suffering. The truth is if these people were pretending to be accomplished violinists, physicists, teachers, artists or engineers they'd soon be caught out, but how do we quantify a financial analyst, tax assessor, political advisor, portfolio manager, asset manager, advertising executive etc? These manipulators have completely taken domination of our entire planet's societies, only now their control is supplemented by a devious manipulation of information alongside their willing cohorts that benefit by supporting them.

3 SELF DELUSION

Tribalist Delusion

Let's ponder a European tribalist viewpoint. If someone from outside of your territory moves in then your reaction is to treat them as an invader and you campaign to expel them using territorial tribal rights as your justification. This stance in itself is violated by you personally, as someone who looks exactly like you is exempt from this hostility even if their family has only lived here for a couple of generations from Germany, France, Australia or wherever. If you truly stood by your convictions then if you found that an Asian or Black family had lived here longer than yours then you'd give up your homestead rights to them. Let's imagine that climate change makes large parts of northern

Europe uninhabitable, would you accept your lot or would you expect France, Germany and other countries to accommodate you? Crops fail and your family and friends fall prey to disease, starvation and mob rule but those foreign countries stand by the same code of ethics as yours and reinforce their barriers, how desperately would you act to save your loved ones? What if the whole of Europe became uninhabitable, would you be justified in forcibly imposing yourself in Asian lands? Imagine that it was found that Negroid peoples arrived in Europe thousands of years before us, would you accept that they're the true occupiers and give them preference? If it was scientifically proven that Asian or Negroid peoples were genetically stronger, superior would you accept that evidence, or would you only accept it if it was in your favour? This isn't just a white or European delusion, peoples all across the planet aren't demanding equality, they're demanding that their own personal tribe be given greater recognition! We have a brutal Israeli regime committing atrocities against Palestinians, but the truth of the matter is that if the shoe was on the other foot the world would be campaigning to prevent atrocities by Palestinians against Israeli's! The list of this twisted logic employed by tribalist manipulators and their willing followers just goes on and on, usually sanitised using language like patriotism or nationalism to lend a veneer of authenticity and justification to their selfist, tribalist madness.

Cognitive Dissonance

Among members of society are people who could be diagnosed as psychopaths. Now the naive belief we've come to identify this condition with relates to people with a savage, ruthless streak and a tendency towards callous violence and murder. This again is our prehistoric tendency to reduce things we don't fully understand to a simplistic model of good and evil. Although this condition may well lead to such brutal outcomes given exceptional circumstances, this seemingly inevitable outcome is far from true, and although relatively small in number a larger proportion of our citizens than we ever imagined have this condition. The main symptom of this condition is a lack of empathy. For the vast majority of us if we saw someone in a supermarket isolated and obviously upset we'd instantly feel distress on their behalf, and either do something ourselves or alert someone who could help. We'd feel compassion. These psychopaths have to exist within our wider community, which often proves difficult for them as they still have the two evolutionary urges but they aren't connected into empathy the way the rest of society is. Narcissism is often a trait they display, not having the subtle social understanding learned by the majority of us to outwardly fully suppress any feelings of superiority. In order to assimilate they have to learn to mimic expressions and attitudes that they see in the people around them depending on their degree of psycopathy, and learn how to manipulate those 'weaknesses' to their own advantage. So for instance cutting into the flesh of someone to perform surgery requires a certain degree of empathetic distance, it certainly doesn't mean that these people who comprise significant positions within our society are dangers to the public, far from it, if we didn't have these people to perform certain jobs then society couldn't function. It's when these people who have learned to mimic the expressions and language of empathy occupy significant civic roles, and in particular positions of political control over us, that we have to be concerned. This dividing line between compassion and a lack of it when manipulated by Tribalists could be seen as being analogous to our psychopathic tendencies being manipulated, only it's worse because a psychopath simply doesn't care, whereas a Tribalist actively has aggression towards their chosen target. Our perception of the world around us is largely still interpreted by that hunter-gather, and cognitive abilities are only now starting to take us further beyond simply surviving, but the beast's understanding of its wider environment can easily be deceived. It's long been acknowledged that humans will subconsciously disregard evidence to avoid painful memories, or to reduce their environment to an overly simplistic model in order to comfort them or make sense of it as a coping strategy. This coping model is an illogical acceptance which denies even absolute evidence in order to simplify their world view and is known as cognitive dissonance. Religion is an easy distraction from either the horrors or simply boredom of life, and once there's no practical alternative it's a particularly attractive distraction. If you hear devoutly religious people speaking you'll hear their language is a bizarre confusion of sentences employed as static to blank out any challenges to their logic and focus them onto a path they've stumbled onto through desperation, frighteningly hostile to any notion that this path is illogical or impractical. If you listen for instance to the followers of Charles

Manson you get these nonsensical ramblings like "We just became Charlie and Charlie became us" and then "Charlie died for us many times". Manson adopted behaviour typical of religious indoctrination through control games, like getting his 'disciples' to take drugs and simulate dying, whereupon they'd be given a new name by him once they came round. They even spoke of him performing miracles, using group reinforcement to consolidate their stories until they became beliefs. The ridiculous situation occurs where religious believers relentlessly demand 100% proof of scientific evidence from physicists who oppose their beliefs, yet they have no proof criteria whatsoever for their own beliefs, and even if they were presented with 100% proof they still wouldn't believe it, ultimately resorting to the trump card of 'faith'.

This religious tribalism has been a relentless feature of our culture in organised societies, and connects into a myriad of perceptive delusions like Stockholm syndrome or simple urban myth sharing. It's indeed sad that people are reduced to this, but a responsible leadership wouldn't utilise this naivety for their own ends with a cocktail of neo-religious scripture and ritual as reinforcement in the form of media control where the message has to be communicated simply and within strict controllable boundaries. It's easy to see how people can be controlled, as you're reading this you may automatically switch to conspiracy theory mode which is how we've been programmed to react and just write me and anyone else who challenges the established order off as some disillusioned crackpots. In the back of our minds surely we must all feel at some instinctive level that the world we were born and coerced into isn't the truth we were led to believe? Consequently the greed elite fear this germ of dissent and will react ruthlessly to stifle it. In the main though the simplistic view most people tend to reduce their world to is that we live in an almost perfect society, and each time there's an election it's just a case of deciding whether it's the red team or the blue team we want to 'tweak' that system a little, and that's the world we're encouraged to see. It's in this contemporary day-to-day life where dominant Tribalists will utilise any and every trickery or brutality in order to maintain their superiority and encourage this view, with the relatively quietened voices of compassion and reason that pose a threat to that way of life ruthlessly stifled.

4 THE RIGGED SYSTEM

Selfism in Action
So let's look at how this deception is maintained at a nuts and bolts level to the ultimate benefit of a greed elite. One thing to remember is that these Tribalists aren't plotting conspiracies in smoke-filled back rooms, they're simply following what they see as a natural instinct. To a degree religious Tribalism still plays a role, although it's largely restricted to small groups spread out randomly across the planet, but still it doesn't take a great deal of insight to see that individual tyrants trigger weapons like Islam, Judaism, Christianity the list goes on, in societies across the globe in order to achieve their personal goals, all purporting to be in the name of a people or

tribe. The overall international secular power base is just a more intricate and carefully constructed machine along the same lines. We could see this power structure internationally as a pyramid, with the greed elite at the top. In order to reward their underlings near the upper part of the pyramid this greed elite needs to set in place a system that their benefactors will want to 'conserve' as part of their selfism and legacy urges. At the top level this allegiance is easily maintained, where the huge spoils of historic land grabs are passed onto subsequent generations and consequently they're the easiest to keep on board, the aristocracy. There'll always be individuals who are simply motivated by greed regardless of the cost to anyone else, and so these entrepreneur's vanity will keep them in the fold believing themselves to be somehow chosen within their society along with the greed elite and aristocracy above them. As the pyramid works its way down we come to the professional and executive classes, where their legacy can be passed on in the form of paid health, education and the law, mainly via a university education and this strata encompasses the mandarins of the pseudo sciences – finance, marketing and politics. The overall result of this system is that the people with wealth will keep it forever and hand it on, and the vast majority of the rest of us will never be allowed to rise above our current station. Entrepreneurs will fluctuate, as the system will always reward someone who makes a rich person even richer, and conservative politicians will change because they emerge from various backgrounds to preach the message of their establishment sponsors. The message must always be that this is 'our' society or 'our' way of life, and anyone who dares to challenge that must obviously be a despicable traitor to 'us'.

Government in the Shadows
We can see how governments have historically been constructed by looking at a contemporary organisation in microcosm, the organised crime syndicate. At the head is a boss who must keep the whole organisation happy in order to consolidate his grip on power. He has under bosses and capos who in turn control parts of the structure beneath them, and the boss knows that he must be vigilant as any of those under bosses will usurp his power given the chance. The further down the chain of command you go the less reward there is, although proportionately even those lesser rewards are still immense in comparison with

people outside of the organisation. Strict checks and controls are in place to ensure that only the authorized person can plunder that particular greed pot, right down to the lowly street runner. In the past there were established titles given to consolidate under bosses' power like bishop, earl, baron etc, that have now been replaced largely by the aptly ecclesiastical minister, or stately senator, but essentially it operates in much the same way. The main difference today is that the real tyrants live in the shadows and allow their avaricious underlings in conservative governments to play out their politician's selfish theatre (show biz for ugly people) and reap the proportionately huge benefits, with these publicity whores acting as a public shield on behalf of their masters.

In antiquity the Roman Empire acted strangely in a naively benign way within a fledgling world of barbaric, uncultured, lawless lands. In one sense they could be seen as introducing a form of education and law to hitherto lawless societies, but all the while enforcing their brutal rule on the rest of the known world. They came to a compromise utilising a system referred to as Pax Romana, where essentially the known world would be governed by the Senate indirectly through deals made with conquered lands. The rulers of these lands were allowed to practice their tyranny without interference from Rome as long as they paid their dues and didn't step out of line, even being recognised as friends and citizens of the Empire. This relieved the pressure on Rome to constantly defend their borders against potentially hostile peoples with the agreement of their own oppressors, in essence bringing these peoples under the Eagle's wing. Today practically nothing has changed, but instead of a Pax Romana we have a Pax Americana, only instead of having cultural, civilized advances as a legacy of that Empire they're indoctrinated into the shallow, greed-driven hedonistic ownership cult of Capitalism. The brutalities are still common, but are now a more hidden, discreet feature of this rule, only now they have developed a most significant weapon in their armoury borrowed and twisted from the Greeks to maintain this power over the people they subjugate, and has become their equivalent of acquiring the atom bomb - Democracy.

Democracy

I can illustrate how modern Democracy works with another analogy. Let's say you, along with a group of parents want to set up a football club for your children. Now your group works all day and you haven't the necessary know-how to run it anyway, so you need someone to do it for you. You narrow it down to four candidates that I've prepared for you to choose from, but you've never met them before. No one questions why it's me who has to narrow down a list of candidates for you to choose you just accept that you're getting a balanced choice. I tell you how one of these candidates would be perfect and I even bring along a colleague who, not only confirms my choice, but also gives strong reasons why the other candidates would be wholly inappropriate, so naturally my candidate gets selected. You're shocked when six months later you find that he's run away with the funds and it also turns out he's a predatory paedophile whose done time for fraud! How could this have happened? You acted on the information you were given, but who gave you that information, did they have anything to gain from it and did you check the validity of the information you were given in the first place? Propaganda has to be controlled by the greed elite in the same way in order for this contrived version of Democracy to work for them, otherwise they'd find another weapon to use. The concept of a vote per citizen is flawed anyway, as how can the ordinary man or woman in the street have the necessary knowledge and expertise to make a logical, reasoned decision, even in the most Utopian of societies? If you took a sick relative to hospital would you take the advice of the medical staff or would you conduct a poll among the entire hospital including cleaning, administration and security staff? When the Democratic system was devised by the Greeks it wasn't meant to be a vote by each person, it was designed for the ruling heads to veto small, powerful interest groups taking disproportionate control. The modern reincarnation of Democracy when in the hands of the greed elite is simply domination by consent, but it's come to be exploited by them as a badge of freedom of choice and liberty. The houses of western parliaments, far from being a stalwart of integrity are simply a leash to hold the status quo, where for instance several childish stalling tactics are used to delay changes to the system, analogous to playing the ball into the corner in football, and even if changes are won in one house there's a second house stocked with aristocrats and conservative peers who will veto them. They're less a ship of state and more a West End farce played out in public at our expense.

Contemporary Selfism
Today more than ever in my lifetime there's a cult of selfishness that is subliminally endorsed and encouraged. This feeds off a growing culture of an attitude of "What's in it for me?" rather than "What's in it for us?", where when you walk through a supermarket someone will be wandering oblivious or just stop, and if it makes you bump into them it's your fault! The same is true with driving, where no one signals or they signal as they move and anything is treated with litigation to get as much compensation as they can. People who have dogs think that the world should defer to dog owners, horse riders feel that it's them, and cyclists or joggers will assume the same attitude. Similarly our media devices are tailored to a regime of advertising ourselves for wanton personal popularity as we're indoctrinated into a cult of watching harrowing events and being unaffected by them because they don't involve us personally, even filming people in distress rather than helping. All the while the interests of people have to be shallow and none thought provoking, so that instead of using this wonderful media for information it's simply relegated to being another tool with which to advertise ourselves. So people will vote for someone who tells them they can keep

more of their 'hard earned' money regardless of other manifesto pledges like reducing healthcare, benefits and pensions, tax relief to the super rich etc. When we're prompted to put our cross on that voting sheet it's even accepted that each person will make a decision based on their own personal gain regardless of the consequences to the wider community, and journalists interviewing voters will report on this as though it's morally acceptable and understandable to do so! Because responsible governance involves consideration and thinking about consequences it's obvious that shallow, more gullible, selfish elements of the electorate will simply vote for jam today, so whoever controls the media controls Democracy. When Putin was accused of interfering in American politics he countered by saying – everyone does it, even you. To which the Americans responded – Ah but we're allowed to because we're spreading Democracy! It's this veneer of credibility that the magic word Democracy evokes that gives the greed elite its credible mandate, and has become the new Christ figure, a banner under which all good and righteous people must gather.

America in particular has a history of interfering with their supposedly sacrosanct credo of respecting the democratic wishes of peoples throughout the world where their own national security is concerned, installing brutal governments via the back door against the 'democratically' elected one. They've exercised financing far right political groups, irrespective of their human rights record, bribed, kidnapped and even murdered and financed wars in order to maintain their stranglehold on the international stage. The illusion has to be maintained at the highest level starting with their own domestic audience, where black Presidents are a sop to the disquiet of African Americans. It doesn't get reported widely that Obama's term spoke a lot but achieved practically nothing, and do his supporters ask themselves why, if he was supposed to truly be a progressive did he then support Clinton over Sanders? Many people outside of America don't realise that their president who is generally lauded with a most progressive term, Lincoln, was actually a Republican, and it goes to show the minimal differences between their parties as opposed to the public perceptions. The contemporary Democrats are simply a diluted alternative of the establishment stranglehold to give the impression that Americans have a credible alternative, allied with an indoctrinated fear response to words like communism or socialism (thank you Josef Stalin *spits*). American 'liberal' talk show programmes speak about Democratic administrations in glowing terms, as though they're a radical alternative to the Republican mindset, again lending the illusion that they have balance and free speech. We now find a character at the helm whose public persona couldn't be more different, yet again all we get is shocking rhetoric but nothing changes. All the while the same song plays it's just the singers who change.

So here we have, in the twenty first century, the apex predator with its tribal elite using their animal instincts to maintain their power and possessions at the cost of the rest of their tribe. In effect we have no direction and have simply abandoned the utopian goals of social reform because we have allowed the rise of selfish manipulators rather than compassionate thinkers. It's vital to these manipulators that the vast majority of us fighting for our existence at the base of this pyramid don't get to see the realities of its structure, so the main barrier that's been established between us and them are the pseudo sciences created as a consequence of the Tribalist regime.

The Pseudo Sciences

Just as in the old world where the church was the mask of the greed elite, so now the structures of finance, marketing and politics fulfil the same role. A serf would have no concept of the logic of how a bishop or vicar functioned during their daily routines, how could they there wasn't any. The ecclesiastical duties were simply the routine maintenance of a system that relied on the division of various groups along Tribalist lines. This suited religious leaders who 'defended' their flocks against rival belief systems with a smorgasbord of abstract rituals and language, and today the pseudo sciences have taken their place, where the mechanics of a society designed to keep us in our place are obscured by strange technical sounding languages and customs. Ask yourself the question, why do we need politics, finance, trade and banking? Well ultimately all of these cathedrals exist because of one thing – seeing ourselves as being a separate, identifiable, individual group. From the time we're old enough we're indoctrinated into seeing ourselves as guests in this machine, and are grateful for the smallest crumbs our 'hosts' deem we deserve, and so this illusion is further reinforced by these groups using this significant barrier created by them to portray their system as scientific. This Tribalist doctrine has divided us into categories where we have to negotiate trade deals with rival groups, or arrange border controls because one group has greater precedence over another. Through property legacy some groups control land and finance and we have to organise deals in order to borrow money from them. As a result of this we have a bizarre neo religious hierarchy, where mathematical equations determine whether or not you can acquire property, strange new languages describe difficulties in free movement or psychological factors can be used to make us choose between commodities and goods. Just as the church did in the past it casts a veil over the workings of the machine we were born into and encourages us to see the mandarins of these pseudo sciences as practicing an art we don't understand. We even have university and college courses to indoctrinate a whole new breed of willing acolytes into this church to preach the Capitalist ethic. So just as we did with the church we allow bankers, ministers, marketing and sales executives, stockbrokers etc, to control it without asking ourselves the significant question – should they exist in the first place? It's in this way the professional strata keep their legacy and hand it on, by becoming executives of the pseudo sciences mostly via the path of university education. These people are about as far from being artistic or scientific as you could possibly be, but they've created this persona where they share the stage with people we'd genuinely respect like engineers, scientists and philosophers. So this system of smoke and mirrors works with the vast majority of the population and serves as a stick to beat any dissenters with. Just as with the older models of Feudalism where the serfs subconsciously were aware of the deception but allowed themselves to be controlled as a way of coping, so today once the majority are brainwashed into acceptance of this hierarchal structure any voices of disquiet have to be stifled. The professional classes play a major role in this as an accessory, remember this isn't a contrived plot but more an acquired instinct to accept and reinforce a system that maintains their privileged role.

5 CONDITIONING THE SLAVES

Propaganda

I'm reminded of the scenario in Pierre Boulle's Planet of the Apes, where humans have lost their intelligence and short-sighted Gorilla's exemplify a brutal view of a future anti-Human society, with Chimpanzees and Oran Utans controlling the civic and educational arena. In one scene a human who's travelled from the past is put on trial as a freak and therefore a threat to the established order for showing intelligence. In order to demonstrate this freak's obvious lack of intelligence he's asked "Tell the court, what is the second article of faith?" to which the 'accused' has to admit he knows nothing of their culture and writings. The accuser triumphantly has the man quietened before long to prevent him responding too vigorously outside of the narrow topic and challenge the court's pre-arranged outcome. I doubt very much that anything I've talked about so far has been a huge surprise, and never having read Marx or any other political philosophers I suspect I'm probably re-hashing an old story. Maybe an old man's focused your mind on particular aspects though, and you might start to wonder why other victims of this oppression who've had the time to consider these aspects and organise haven't done anything about it. Believe me they've tried and are still trying! Even the most naive and gullible members of our society would rebel against this oppression if the whole truth was laid bare in front of them, so the most significant ammunition in the armoury of this greed elite which has to be used in conjunction with Democracy has been the control of the agenda. In the past our experience of the world was through direct contact, albeit augmented with hearsay and limited personal opinions of others, but as technology has advanced mass media has replaced our more direct experience of the world with one that exists more in images and messages piped into us from whoever controls this technology. Just as the feudal overlords augmented their support with religious iconography and subliminal messages, so the mass media can now much more efficiently supplant their chosen narrative into our subconscious, with the first rule of propaganda being to only allow topics to be introduced that are none threatening to the status quo. At one time the control of these topics was relatively easy, where the only real outlet for protest was via the pulpit or at the theatre, but as we moved into the nineteenth and especially the twentieth century newspapers and radio became a loose cannon the greed elite had to take a more subtle control over. Political awakening in the modern era has its roots in thinkers such as Hegel and Kant, and were expanded on with reference to our industrialised world through the writings of people like Marx and Engels where the ordinary men and women in the street started to think seriously about the imbalances in their societies.

Possibly the most insidious character in attempts to free ourselves of these chains was Josef Stalin. Once his political adversaries such as Lenin and Trotsky were removed from the picture he hijacked the ideas the rebellion was based on to cement his validity by using the icons of Marx and others to justify his rule in the same way as American presidents have hijacked the Founding Father's constitution. This psychopathic tyrant headed a vicious Tribalist dictatorship for decades. Not only did he give the greed elite in the West the perfect bogey man to scare their populations with, but also the writings of Marx and Engels will forever be emblematic with this monster. The term 'Marxist' has become as wicked an expression in the same way as the term 'Democracy' has become a term of sanctuary. The real origins of propaganda in the modern era start with the Soviet Union but began to be honed by the German propaganda ministry of Josef Goebbels in the 1930's. We can see how powerful a device propaganda has grown to become very graphically by examining this process in action in recent history with reference to their practitioners. In 1944 in Germany a group of senior army officers attempted to assassinate Adolf Hitler during a briefing. There was a network in place ready to communicate between the plotters, but the plot failed. Goebbels, who ran the Nazi propaganda machine had laughed on hearing of the failure, saying that if it had been organised by him he would simply have seized control of the radio and newspapers and spread lies to galvanise rebellion. In 1944 newspapers and radio were relatively sparse in comparison to the ever present, often intrusive multi-media we experience today and anyone who doesn't realise how this weapon of choice is being utilised by the bad shepherds is being naive in the extreme. Even with wildly fantastic scenarios people will be susceptible to believing them. Orson Welles had broadcast his namesake's 'War of the Worlds' fiction just a few years earlier causing hysteria amongst some American listeners, illustrating the extent to which an audience can be fooled. When the Nazi regime was planning a campaign of extermination on groups such as gypsies and those with mental disorders as well as Jews, Goebbels propaganda ministry produced a film in 1941 "Ich klage an" or "I Accuse". The story was about a seemingly educated doctor whose wife was terminally ill and dying in pain. The husband ends his wife's life and is subsequently put on trial, at which point the remainder of the film is a back and forth debate concerning the justification of mercy killing and euthanasia. Now it's important to emphasise that the German people were just people like you and me, even though our own contemporary propaganda needed to put a different slant on this, the fact is that they were manipulated in the same way that Tribalists had always done and are still doing to this day. Our own post war film industry was awash with more subtle undertones in films like "The Cruel Sea" where officers were middle class barristers and the like, but the cannon fodder was the working class man in the street who doffed his cap in deference to his 'betters' and the enemy was a faceless threat to 'our' way of life. In the 1960 election in the USA John Kennedy narrowly took victory from Richard Nixon universally regarded as being largely due to the success of his TV appearance. A perfect illustration of the power of the imagery of visual media is that the people who listened on the radio thought that Nixon had won the debate. So we can see what considerable power is in the hands of the people running these broadcasts. Haven't you ever wondered why billionaires want to acquire media outlets?

History has a tendency to be written by its winners, consequently the relentless fallacy is one of being a citizen of an evolved, ordered, just, evolving society where near perfection simply needs to be tweaked towards the ultimate goal of Utopia. This illusion has to be scrupulously maintained by willing accessories, not secretive plotters, to the 'conservation' of their system and any debates rely on using the starting point that this is the way it is and it just needs organising. The debate is then hijacked using pseudo science rhetoric to confuse any challenges and keep it under their control. If these conservatives had to rely on morality alone then their argument would collapse. We all have vague recollections of events from our early childhood, but most of us will have the more fully developed memories from about the age of eight or so. I think we all have that feeling deep down that we're still that eight year old child, but life experience has taught us to become hardened to the realities of the world, and so in large part we act the way we feel is expected, will protect or won't upset those we care or feel responsible for. This insecurity will vary depending on how safe and secure your environment is, the more secure you feel the more you identify with the system that gives you that security, but the less secure you are the more vulnerable certain elements could become to rebelling, and so propaganda is mostly directed at these sections of society. If you really examine how you view the world from an early age, think about it. I'm sure we all have that indoctrinated feeling that the people running this huge machine somehow have a gift, a talent that we don't really get but accept it because they're above us in the chain controlling this strange machine so it must be the case. It's only when we interact with these people as individuals that we realise they're simply ordinary people like us, it's just they got lucky in the lottery of life, or more accurately the system. Do you see how the pseudo sciences fool us, casting a veil over simplicity and enforce the feeling that we're just not as enlightened or tuned-in as the benefactors of our wonderful society? Whether it be the property developer, Conservative politician, accountant, marketing executive etc, we're all given our pseudo science catch phrases and equations. We're bemused by a strange language of statistics that rely on other statistics, compounded by neo-scientific catch phrases that are usually abbreviated or have initials to stand for them. As we watch these elevated members of our government along with political and social commentators it's as if they pay lip service to allowing us to hear, or even comment on their wise pronouncements as they pat us on the head and expect we'll just leave them to it. It's worse when they challenge someone in the street to comment on some abstract element of foreign or fiscal policy, where the person will pretend they understand this bizarre Newspeak and so reinforce the message to the viewer that we should just leave it to the experts ... ."Tell the court, what is the second article of faith?". In an ideal responsibly administered world we as citizens would play a limited executive role in civic responsibility, but as we've been manipulated to become pawns in a game of democratic pretence we're relentlessly conditioned into allying ourselves with our perceived benefactors. Some of us will assert our beliefs and opinions much more resolutely than others even if our knowledge of it is limited, this isn't necessarily through a lack of intelligence but partly through personality and a sense of perceived duty. How the manipulators practice their craft will adapt to appeal more efficiently to target demographics (apologies for the pseudo-science Newspeak). It's been said that good design is that which isn't noticed, and among the professional classes there is the structure of the media, with film, TV and newspapers, and recently the advent of social media which is more of a challenge for them to control. Social media however has the convenient aspect of dubious credibility, being an unregulated forum for anyone and everyone and it remains to be seen how this media will be adapted by the greed elite.

Propaganda Today

So once we've been coerced into accepting this model we have to be kept subservient, and this is achieved by a drip feed of propaganda. As an example the most abstract of the pseudo sciences is advertising. Executives and entrepreneurs preach bizarre tracts that appeal to that avarice in us and also their followers who have aspirations of becoming like them. They're essentially just made up as they go along, and are therefore ideally suited to entertainment platforms. Although I never watched a particular programme I've seen enough clips to get the gist of it, it was called 3-2-1 with Ted Rodgers. The contestants were presented with riddles so abstract that the solution could be interpreted as anything from "The Cat sat on the Mat" to "Power to the People" and has become famous for this farcical concept. A contemporary programme illustrates the same ridiculous nature of the pseudo science of business and marketing "The Apprentice UK". A collection of eager acolytes hang on every word of the entrepreneur Alan Sugar, seemingly oblivious to the concept being played out in plain sight that the coveted prize is a disgusting financial reward, with the contestants being no more than a collection of shallow, narcissistic materialists who stab each other in the back, pose, lie and cheat. It's never questioned that the production of meaningless trinkets and the like are pedaled to a gullible consumer market in order to bring personal wealth of inordinate proportions to individuals without the conscience to care who suffers as a consequence. In one episode Sugar might reward a contestant for earning more money, but in another will reward someone for a completely contradictory result. Both Sugar and the viewers bask in the delusion that these pearls of wisdom are some kind of scientific discipline and highlight how we're fooled into blind acceptance of this concept simply because we don't understand it but neither do we question it. Remembering that old adage that good design is that which isn't noticed, then similarly successful propaganda won't stand out, so TV programmes like The Apprentice and Dragon's Den with their increasingly ridiculous theatrical pitch stunts parade this unjust system in plain sight and become accepted. Another device is a programme called "Undercover Boss" where the CEO of a company is disguised and sent into the workplace in a subterfuge pretending to be a lowly worker, mingling with various employees at the bottom rung of the ladder.

The climax is the reveal, where this mysterious person they've been working with is shown to actually be their exalted God-like leader. We experience a cathartic show of tears and understanding as this mandarin sees the error of his ways and his workers now see this figure as one of the boys, suddenly everything is wonderful with the capitalist world again. Of course we can't all identify with entrepreneurs and business executives, so we're subdued by reality shows and quizzes that give out vast rewards along with lotteries, allowing us to dream that one day we too can become part of this limited inheritance cult. We have consumer programmes where experts advise us on how to avoid falling prey to these sanctioned sharks who are legally allowed to rob us through a variety of carefully constructed con tricks, treating it as if it's simply part of life and if we don't take advice from these TV experts then we've only ourselves to blame! In-between everything we're bombarded with commercials advising us how we can avoid falling prey to these sharks by allying ourselves with other sharks, each character either smiling out at you as your friend or grimacing as your wicked enemy with whichever music they think will fool you. How can we possibly be fooled by a system that actually promotes gambling with incentives to lull you in? When it's become part of the propaganda anything's possible!

One of the most engaging formats appeals to the selfism in us at a more identifiable level. "Homes under the Hammer" parades the system in its bare bones, where you don't even need to be particularly innovative or a selfish shark as in the other example shows. If you've managed to acquire enough money, sometimes as an entrepreneur but mostly through savings as an employee of one of the pseudo sciences, then this is the scam for you. A property is walked through, usually dilapidated, with the light-hearted commentary dismissing its condition as something like "Well this property could certainly use a bit of tlc" as the jolly music plays in the background. It side-steps the entire back story completely of a succession of families who've desperately tried to make ends meet, ploughing their hard earned money into trying to make a home. Finally they either die or are evicted at which point bankers, property speculators and landlords pick over it like a carcass leaving our hero to step in. We put the previous owners out of our mind completely as we identify with this budding entrepreneur looking to make a profit of thousands. There's an uncomfortable acceptance of the numbers involved as the expert first explains to the audience that this is small potatoes at the lower income end of the market. Our buyer says "Well we've spent £70,000 and we reckon we can do the renovations for about another £9,000". Our resident expert shakes their head and says "Well I think you need to be more realistic and think of nearer £17,000" while the vast majority of us watching are just about managing to survive with no savings or pension plans. The decisions then move through how to make the most profit out of any potential buyers. Should we divide it up into separate units and choose multiple targets, or just make one palatial property and try to make a killing on that? At the end of the programme everyone's won, or maybe on very rare occasions broken even, illustrating that if you've got money to start with you can always make more out of the rest of us. We seem to be so distracted by empathising with this property speculator , who seems so much like us, that we completely forget we're watching a money-go-round that we'll never be able to take part in ...because we haven't got any money to start with!

Rules of their Game
Propaganda follows two basic principles (Rule number 1) *Control the agenda*. This is pretty

self explanatory, it doesn't matter what's happening in the world, if you don't know about it then it doesn't exist, and if you're not allowed to even discuss it then how can it be addressed. Unless you hear about it directly then it might as well not be happening at all, and in a world of billions of inhabitants the only real way to hear of it is through controlled outlets. This is easy in the case of pre-recorded dramas, quizzes, sitcoms and even documentaries, but requires subtlety when purporting to present topical subjects. At any one time somewhere on the planet someone will be committing tribalist/selfist crimes, whether it's atrocities, exercising political corruption or abusing their power in some other way, where unscrupulous 'leaders' extort billions from their now poor citizens. With a large panorama of events it's relatively easy to justify which stories are prioritised and which are ignored completely, and there's always the human interest angle where attention can be focused on a unique fashion craze or a humorous video that's gone viral, particularly useful as an upbeat summary to reassure you that everything's still fine with the world. The lowest form of journalism however is the fabrication of reality, where something innocuous can be blown out of proportion or even completely manufactured by interested parties. Even if these stories are openly proven to be false human nature will retain them as 'There's no smoke without fire'. The perceived role of journalists has become practically irrelevant and is more akin to sponsored establishment commentator.

(Rule number 2) *Establish your Characters*. In order for your audience to accept your message they must have characters they can identify with and who are seen as a moral compass through which we interpret the unfolding story. Just as Goebbels used his benign doctor as a standard to unite behind and Stalin used soldiers of the 'Marxist' cause in dramatic re-enactments, so film and TV use the same devices. The characters and the subjects discussed must be designed as near as possible to have no middle ground and simply prompt you to decide whether you're with us or against us. They can be used to reinforce their view of a way of life, or even twist reality, for instance historical failures can be turned around to appear as triumphs as in Scott of the Antarctic or Dunkirk, or much more subtly these days to establish the validity of the status quo through the well established sitcom format.

The sitcom's success as an engaging format is obvious in the fact that nostalgia channels still air, not only contemporary shows, but also historic episodes. For those of you my age do you remember a sitcom called The Good Life? As a naive teenager I'd laugh along with the antics of a self-sufficiency couple Tom and Barbara who were 'rebelling against the system'. There were hilarious antics with their Conservative neighbour's contrasting lifestyles in Margot and Jerry and one episode caused a profound awakening in me. There was a titled lord at the time who, because of his social conscience and political convictions renounced his title and seat in the House of Lords in order to campaign on behalf of the less fortunate in society. Sir Anthony Wedgewood-Benn (Tony Benn) was a man of impeccable principles as shown by his actions and words, and consequently was an immense threat to the greed elite of the time. This particular episode involved Tom and Barbara's livestock contracting fleas, and the subsequent social stigma of how to keep Margot and Jerry away. They discussed a potential subterfuge where Tom suggested "We could always tell Margot we've got Michael Foot staying with us for the week". Now this was a genuinely humorous line as Michael Foot was the Labour Party leader at the time and Margot was a staunch Conservative. The thing that really brought reality home was when Barbara continued dramatically "Oh Tom I've just had an even more horrible thought" to which Tom responded "Wedgy Benn?" before she continued with a qualification to her point. Not only was the line deliberately contrived for you to accept the premise as acceptable, being sanitised through the characters we were expected to identify with, but there was also a pause allowed where the audience could not only laugh loudly but actually applaud. We therefore by association start to accept Margot's justification in seeing her domestics taking holidays as the thin end of the wedge, or Jerry fiddling his expense account as just a typical, accepted part of executive life. It's humorous when Margot is shocked that an Asian family might be moving in next door to her because we can identify with that right? We're shown members of the aristocracy who are 'one of the people' and work hard, policemen, window cleaners and postmen happily accepting their lot. This format is a direct descendant of the wartime propaganda dramas and the success of propaganda like this is in its subtlety which infects every nook and cranny of the information being drip fed to us through an ever-expanding entertainment medium. The sitcom became an accepted formula with which to reinforce the idea of middle class stereotypes, where professional people live in large houses, working class people accept their poverty and the status quo is the model of perfection and contentment. Just as with news media they're selective with which topics they introduce and how they present them, fabricating and embellishing story lines to lead you in the direction they want you to follow. The script writers, producers and directors aren't huddled in dark rooms plotting, they're simply following their instincts that ultimately 'conserve' their privileged situation. The important message they have to instill into us as background music is that it's still 'our' country or 'our' way of life. Topical panel shows, in my opinion, are our only chink of light where we're allowed the illusion of expressing our feelings. I see it as being let out into the exercise yard before being incarcerated once more, and these stand-up comedians allow us a scant view from the abyss so long as they don't wander too far outside of the boundaries. They also provide a veneer of credibility that we're allowed free speech.

Hollywood can basically get away with murder, after all it's known as the Dream Factory and we understand it is as a series of independently funded ventures anyway. Whereas the light entertainment medium can be seen as indirect indoctrination it's when we come to what we're led to believe are factual news programmes that our conformity is really controlled as this medium is instilled into us as representing the real world. Discussion and debating programmes are seen as a shining example of open government, because they appear to allow the illusion that anything can be added to the agenda and aired in a public forum. These forums are used to hide the reality that society is a carefully constructed machine that's presented as being almost perfection, with any allowable discussions aimed at how to tweak it a little. The pre-set topics for discussion will only be those that stay within the accepted agenda spectrum, and any variance from these specific subjects will be skillfully guided away or terminated by the arbitrator with the added credibility of being introduced initially by invited audience members in the first place. Consequently an easy way to shut down any unwanted line of debate is simply to say "We can discuss that at another time, however we're going to stick to the question being asked", usually followed by prompting another audience member to contribute and bring the discussion back in the intended direction. The conservative representatives on these panels will relentlessly trigger Tribalist cooperation from the more gullible members of the audience by regularly climaxing their statements and speeches with words such as "British" or frightening them with words like "Lefty" or as in a contemporary constructed fiction "Anti-Semite" . Because their arguments are principally immoral and selfist then their case would collapse if the issues were reduced to basic morality, so they have to either stoop to base tribalism or drag any arguments back to present day where they can cloud the issue with pseudo science mumbo jumbo – trade deficits, financial percentages etc. Just as with the sitcom format the chairman will be a familiar figure with whom we identify and therefore trust their arbitration. Remember that all these contributors aren't plotters, rather they're willing participants in a system that supports their personal security and so has come to embody their value system. It's when we move into the realm of private propaganda mediums that we can really feel the spores of that dystopian virus infecting society. If you see the contemporary Russian propaganda machine at work it's easy to see the lessons Putin's ministry has learned from the West, and unless you heard them speaking Russian with Cyrillic sub titles you'd be hard pushed not to think that the presenters and political commentators speaking benignly out at you were simply a new Sky TV channel. It's only when you see their Dictator being presented on what ostensibly appears to be a panel discussion show threatening that any traitors will "Kick the bucket" that you realise how crafted and subtle our own social propaganda is. The sale of this private propaganda machine to unscrupulous billionaires with their 'Divine' agenda is moving Capitalism in the West into ever more dangerous territory.

6 DIVIDE AND RULE

National and International News (Our biggest enemy)

From the time we're old enough to sense the world we become willing participants with the information box in our homes. It entertains us, educates us and most significantly 'informs' us. We probably interact with it more than even our closest friends or family, and as such its characters with which we become familiar are not only its children's presenters, but also as we grow with it its news presenters too. The legitimacy this brings can't be overstated, and even those who pay little direct attention to its reports who largely use social networking entertainment will be indirectly influenced by their wider social network that do. Just as we accept that our close family and friends will have our best interests at heart and won't lie to us, so too we welcome these familiar characters into our world as trusted confidants and advisors. Remember that these journalists and news readers aren't plotting this, they're simply being used as a willing conduit to disseminate their owner's message within the nation state that employs them. Granted there will occasionally be journalists with an independent social conscience, but these renegades will be tolerated and lend that familiar veneer of credibility towards an illusion of balance. Otherwise these journalists are sponsored indirectly by whichever news channel they gravitate towards, and become almost like a familiar guest in your home preaching the Capitalist credo via subliminal suggestions given to them to announce as fact. We perceive these summaries as truth, when in fact they're carefully constructed versions that they want us to see, leaving only one interpretation without having to actually say it. The important thing they have to instill into us is that it's 'our' country or 'our' way of life. Whereas fiction relies on whichever characters the author can create, topical news programmes have the added difficulty of not being able to present constructed, fictitious characters for us to identify with when presenting news items, although news anchors assume a similar role once they've served their time as a journalist in the field. The real life political characters whose images are paraded across our screens have to be subtly morphed into as near pantomime villains or benign benefactors in just the same way as the sitcom format and this 'news' deception is at the vanguard of modern propaganda. If we think of the way advertising works a trustworthy character is portrayed as representing the stance they want you to take, and anyone disputing it is an incompetent, bumbling buffoon. So the call centre agent is a benign, kindly woman telling the caller how their insurance package will guarantee their family's security at such little cost that only the idiot in his garish shirt and out of date hairstyle falling over the clutter in his garage wouldn't go for it. Just as with the discussion show or sitcom format we learn to identify with these familiar mediators, so when the incumbent Tory government leader is referred to with a wistful smile as "Prime Minister" the opposition leader is stoically mentioned as "Mr X". Anyone who speaks out too close to home will immediately be made a target of ridicule (remember Tony Benn) or simply be ignored, but mostly adverse news stories simply won't see the light of day. Little subliminal suggestions are just the tip of a carefully constructed iceberg, with the national order being presented as a state of near perfection with two sides vying for the right to administer it with that ever-present banner of Democracy being the rallying point. The result is that this relentless media reinforcement automatically promotes these conservative oppressors to a level playing field status, so that even if adverse issues that can't be stifled knock them back they still stay near the top of the credibility rankings, and individual inept or scape-goated conservatives are simply retired or given a privileged role within the establishment but away from the limelight.

Controlling the agenda means paying scant regard to any adverse issues or ignoring them altogether. For instance human rights abuses are a relentless feature of our tribalist world, but they're only reported on where that country is standing in the way of our greed elite operating freely there. Atrocities committed by countries that trade with the West are simply ignored or mentioned briefly as though they're casual, routine updates. Another tactic is to have two guests reviewing the papers who appear to have diverse opinions therefore giving the illusion that an alternative viewpoint is put forward. The truth is that their opinions are mostly shifted to the right anyway and the programme pre-recorded, where selected news stories to be discussed will be vetted and the 'mediator' instructed to terminate that line of discussion if it goes the wrong way. One of these news channels has found a way of diverting the agenda and at the same time establishing environmental credibility by promoting a campaign to take used plastics out of the oceans. Not only does this create an image of social conscience, but also it can be reactivated if there aren't genuine news diversions to act as an alternative smokescreen. We aren't talking about plotters in smoke-filled dark rooms planning a hidden strategy, it's the subconscious actions of the mind set of people who, in reality, have little genuine compassion and are following their genetically programmed legacy and selfism urges. The result of all of this is that we're deceived into thinking that we've been given all the facts from a trusted, compassionate source and can now make an informed decision. The important thing they have to instill into us is that it's 'our' country or 'our' way of life.

The World Today

So ultimately where has this cancer of these three primitive urges led? Our entire civilization has been abandoned to opportunists, where not only do we allow their persecution of the rest of society, but also they've ensured that the rules are actually constructed to encourage it and a whole array of pseudo scientific static blots out the true simplicity. It's the reason why most of our children will always scrape a living in low paid work, or even end up homeless while the minority will always have a comfortable or even disgustingly luxurious lifestyle. Why is it that innovative medical equipment and the like isn't developed for the good of the masses but rather the enrichment of individuals? Why don't people see the immorality of charity, where we're asked to contribute from our meagre earnings while our societies are infested with millionaires, billionaires and trillionaires? Why are urgent questions like climate change and overpopulation ignored, smiling as the weather forecast makes light of this heat wave and how we hope it'll continue as we show people eating ice creams in the glorious sunshine? Great growing weather for grapes in our northern European climate as we smile and toast the slow death of our planet. Why do we have to shop around for the best 'deal' for a mortgage, electricity or insurance and even have to pay for water that falls from the sky? The news is deluged with disastrous stewardship of significant privately run civic departments, all the while issuing anonymous written statements in legal mumbo-jumbo excusing yet another calamitous disaster of the system and sacking its perpetrators with a disgustingly large golden handshake. Why are the only people who design our world those who are allowed to filter through this corrupted system rather than an efficient planned design to find each person their niche? If you've ever seen the film "Brazil" it perfectly portrays a society where basic innovations exist, but an antiquated Heath Robinson bureaucracy reveals a nightmarish environment where justifications are made to excuse a broken system where unimaginative manipulators have taken charge, bumbling around trying to make it work like unfocussed children. This disease infects everything, quality of life, engineering, infrastructure, even the arts. Just to take random examples a low budget film was put together in the mid 70's that studio bosses didn't want to back, however this creative crew persevered with their project and Star Wars became probably the most popular

film of all time. Of course once these narrow-
minded, greed-driven studio owners realised
how much money it could make them they
financed a re-hash of the same format over
and over. Meanwhile how many other artistic
projects never saw the light of day because
they needed financing, but the only source of
finance was people with no imagination who
couldn't see how it would make them
immediately richer? How many truly artistic
works rather than populist adventure features
could've been explored? I find it particularly
disturbing when the talents of film makers are
used in advertising, where for instance we're
shown wide-eyed children running down to a
beach with a herd of horses galloping in slow
motion to evocative music, only to find out that
this mysterious, ethereal message is to tell us
how benign and wonderful a banking
corporation is. Recently advances by an
American paleontologist discovered that soft
tissues could well be extracted from fossilised
dinosaur bones, maybe even DNA fragments,
but the fossils themselves are bid against in
international auctions and so are too expensive
to be taken away from exhibits for scientific
research. Research into a cure for breast
cancer was hindered because there were
disputes over patent laws. Animals are being

slaughtered because the prehistoric myths of properties of their bodies create a commercial market. Why was a brand new, expensive national stadium built at Wembley, demeaning the significance of the FA Cup Final by holding the semi's there too? Surely not just so fat cats could administer it and treat it as a precursor to a night out in the West End? The stadium, built with our money, is now under consideration of being 'sold' and I wonder where our money would go? When you buy electrical goods the range is so wide with none standard accessories because individual manufacturers want to hold you to ransom and squeeze as much profit out of it as they can, sales assistants promote their own brands regardless of whether it's a better or more suitable product so that they can earn commission and the list goes on. These are just a tiny part of a multitude of wasted humanity and ingenuity and anyone could sit and tick off scores of examples like these. This crazy system designed by and for low intellect, untalented, greed driven manipulators means that any artistic or scientific breakthroughs are made not because of Capitalism but in spite of it. Probably the saddest failing of this greed driven environment is how our race is being held back technologically, which can be perfectly demonstrated using one particular example contrasting two men's lives at the turn of the twentieth century.

Thomas Edison may indeed have been an innovator, but his innovation wasn't what brought him wealth and influence, his skill lay in organising and manipulating. Now everyone's heard of Edison, he invented the electric light bulb didn't he? Well no he didn't, he actually used clever patents to jointly gain royalties from the man who did improve the light bulb design to how we know it today Joseph Swan, and Edison's wealth came from other patents mostly piggy-backing other inventions such as Marconi's telegraph (which in itself had been hijacked from our second protagonist). When contacted by a Yugoslavian engineer Edison recognised his talent and invited him to join his company with the promise of a huge reward for modifying and improving his electrification system. This young engineer not only improved on but re-designed the system at its most basic level, netting Edison both recognition and reward, after which Edison then refused to pay the engineer the reward promised. That young engineer was a man called Nikola Tesla. When Tesla tried to introduce his safer, more efficient electrification system via George Westinghouse's company

Edison began an active and viscous campaign to discredit it using any underhand methods he could. In later years Tesla would bring to the world innovations of technology that essentially pioneered the technology of the world we know today and even voluntarily waived his royalty dues from Westinghouse to save that company for what he felt was the betterment of science. The potential backers of the socially uncomfortable Tesla were the likes of JP Morgan, who typically had amassed enormous wealth purely by their powers of manipulation and organisation, and only ever committed to financing things that would net them personal profit. In later years Tesla would go cap in hand to Morgan and others for funding of other innovative ideas, but Morgan and his kind being typically unimaginative and greed driven denied him all but scant funding as it didn't swell the coffers of those already obscenely rich industrialists and bankers. One of the innovations he put forward was for an electric car, another project he was working on was wireless, unlimited energy and it makes me mad just writing it but the likelihood is he was deliberately targeted by industry and oil interests to stifle it. It intrigues you to think of the marvellous technological advances our modern day world might've enjoyed had Tesla and his kind been allowed to fulfil their full potential. Edison died wealthy and famous while the pious genius Tesla died practically anonymous.

The Future

These cruel and immoral miscarriages of justice are the hallmark of modern day Capitalism that holds back innovation, because the one and only ultimate motivation is pure, selfish greed. Any society where it's not only acceptable but encouraged to leave an inheritance, by definition can't be an equal society. This mindset that inheritance is acceptable is brainwashed into us, as it's the basis for the perpetration of this crime and is a necessary device of the ruling greed elite. They've ensured through, not just inheritance but also as a consequence control of the media and development of Democracy and the pseudo sciences, that there's a complicated puzzle to confuse and cloud your mind to exactly what the nuts and bolts of the wealth of any society is, as the veils of politics, finance, trade, foreign policy etc, have been deliberately designed to cover up its simplicity and excuse inheritance. Democracy won't last forever, in fact the more enlightened the world is becoming its death knell is being sounded as we speak, and we have to be deeply concerned at the depths this greed elite will sink to in order to maintain their stranglehold over us. World leaders have already started outright lying and even committing murders and abductions in plain view of the world, and when challenged will simply deny accusations with a smug smile, accuse the accusers of being prejudiced or arrogantly dismiss it as 'fake news'. As our jails continue to fill with the victims of this despicable torment, wars rage internationally and the planet is slowly being poisoned by this insidious crime we must prepare for worse to come when these tactics no longer fool enough of us to maintain their control. One nation alone can't banish this wickedness from the Earth because the tentacles of this cancer spread right across it, and any organ that starts to go into remission will be attacked by the host body.

Any beliefs of ridding ourselves of these chains has always been based around playing them at their own game and hoping that common sense would prevail, so that when brave voices of rebellion are rewarded with representation within their democratic farce they see the sense in accepting it. History tells us though that these tyrants would stop at nothing, destroying our entire planet to maintain their position. What can we do? The dilemma is and always has been, how do you fight to install a system of morality and principles against an enemy who has none? If we think of the dock workers in America trying to establish a union, the owners recruited gangster mercenaries to crack heads, and during the 50's the dark menace of 'Communism' was used to subdue any voices of dissent to the defensive post-war American establishment. We'd face the same hostile attacks but on a larger, more frightening scale. How do we begin to spread the message to those blinded by this deception so that this cabal no longer has a stranglehold on the organs of disinformation and we are no longer under their control? Even the tiniest steps seem unattainable in the current climate, but we mustn't be negative. We owe it to our children and the children of generations to come to put an end to this disease now! The meek may inherit the Earth, but the strong have to put them there in the first place.

Let's imagine we have an old Victorian chimney, where the upper quarter or so is unsound but we could re-structure the lower three quarters and transform it into something useful. Placing explosives part way up and allowing the top portion to crash to the ground would risk untold damage to fragile properties surrounding it. Instead you'd have to dismantle it brick-by-brick from the top. These individuals controlling the system wouldn't have a clue how to press the buttons they'd financed to defend themselves, they have their propaganda outlets and armed mercenaries between them and us who are either fooled into believing their controller's world order or understand it but ally themselves with whom they see as their parasitic dependent hosts anyway, largely through cognitive dissonance. Our only avenue of freedom is making these mercenaries realise that, not only are they allying themselves with a despicable enemy, but that they too are part of our larger society and not a guard dog against the very people whose duty it is to protect. We have a historic example a little over a hundred years ago, of a society where masses of people were starving, dying in the streets, where ordinary people couldn't afford to live because all of the fruits of their labours were taken from them and given to a pampered elite who paraded their disgusting wealth in open view of the very people they were stealing it from. It resulted in a desperate rage of rebellion where armed forces consisting of men of those same victims were sent to kill their family and friends in order to maintain that corrupt system. The priority must be to educate these guard dogs from the ground up into allowing a transformation to happen, and not to continue propping up a corrupt, wicked administration from the shadows under the fiction of 'our' country. Do we really want the inevitable rage to result in bloodshed, maybe risking another Stalin hijacking the situation to fill the vacuum or worse, or do we want to have a planned transformation into a Utopian society in a collaborative harmony with each and every citizen? This rage will come, humans can only be pushed so far and when that breaking point comes in this day and age the consequences could be the last chapter in a story that, for all we know, may never have happened before in the Universe or likely to again.

7 EXECUTIVE ACTION

After the Storm
In order to radically change the way we do
things in both quality of life and efficiency it's
vital that we do three simple things, firstly take
a free market economy out of the equation.
Secondly health, education and the Law are
equal for all, there's no necessity to qualify this,
it means exactly what it says, and thirdly
inheritance must be the gift of the state and not
individual citizens. We're all individuals and we
don't want to reduce ourselves to robots and
numbers dressed and speaking the same and
tolerance should be the hallmark. It's obvious
to me that no society could function if each
citizen received the exact same reward, so a
system must encompass a reward mechanism

where strict criteria decides what proportion of our wealth is allocated based on merit, not a variable reward decided by individuals. The human instinct to work and contribute for a proportionate reward has to be built in to any system, but just as important it has to be fair and benefit society as a whole. We cannot again allow a system to benefit some individuals thousands, millions, billions or even trillions of times more than the average citizen, not just for its immorality but also its consolidation of independent power bases acting in selfist Feudal dominance to rise and perpetuate the whole disgusting scenario all over again.

What we may refer to as Capitalism could possibly work in an alternate limited format as long as it was administered and regulated by the state, where individual expertise could be utilised and rewarded but private enterprise would only be allowed on a relatively small scale within a certain sphere and profit ceiling. Every branch of the consumer market at the moment is in direct conflict with every other branch in a selfist battle to gain the highest profit at the expense of, not only their competitors but also as a consequence the consumer and the environment. In a properly run system we still wouldn't all have the same car, vacuum cleaner or washing machine, but more importantly we wouldn't be held hostage by an individual manufacturer, and all development could be in line with environmental conformity rather than by pigs with their snouts in the trough. For any of you thinking "Well it didn't work for the Eastern Block" of course it didn't, it was a sham because it was simply a dictatorship masquerading as socialism, and anyway two factors were against it from the start. One was a tyrant who didn't care about the well being or even the lives of his citizens and simply ran it as a dictatorship, and the other was the fact that the rest of the world blockaded and vilified it in an attempt to further their own brand of tyranny. If a system was regulated by a conscientious state, then in effect nothing would change other than the limits of credit an individual could earn and the restrictions on unnecessary administrators with concocted 'jobs for the boys' titles like chief executive, vice chairman etc. Ultimately it simply means that the wealth created by the workforce doesn't go towards unlimited profit for individuals but rather a regulated system designed for the good of the wider community, and it seems ridiculous that it has to even be pointed out! The biggest share of any individual company's budget is easily the massive wage bill for unnecessary executives, and things like sales, profit and marketing along with other concocted tribalist pseudo sciences would be irrelevant anyway so would be dispensed with. If you try to use the argument that entrepreneurs would relocate to a society where they could reap a larger reward than the generous one granted them from the state then both you and they would be morally bankrupt. Trying to suggest that someone who makes a good living in one society would decide to operate in one that makes them a billionaire tells its own story. How many yachts, houses does anyone need? It also highlights the biggest threat any developing liberation would face from hostile international Tribalists who saw a threat to their privileged tyranny.

One of the biggest benefits to a none 'free market economy' would be the cultivation of genuine talent. An education system would be in place where there were no restrictions to hinder a budding Tesla or Newton. If someone had a penchant as a medical genius, artist or engineer they would be spotted early in their life and sponsored by the state rather than have to fight their way out of slum housing and even then have to again fight for the attention of a greedy entrepreneur or industrialist. A sick mindset of selfists is an innate belief that this is still survival of the fittest, and lip service is paid to the physically handicapped or less intelligent, whereas the opposite is the case. Those of us lucky enough to be able-bodied owe an even greater compassion to our fellow human so that their life can be as fulfilling as we can possibly make it. Everyone, no matter what their physical condition or health would be treated equally and a respectable allocation of the budget would negate the need entirely for charity other than minority interest groups. Families indigenous to their area could stay together rather than being deprived of housing through extortionate competitive fees pricing them out. Hucksters won't be legalised to try and trick vulnerable people out of money via relentless junk calls and other legalised scams, and just because something is popular it won't be sold to someone who can then own it and make a profit from it, rather it would be promoted to the benefit of the wider community. Art would be encouraged as an enlightened pursuit rather than a device to make rich people richer and the working week would be not only more fulfilling but more flexible and even reduced, but significantly innovations would occur with the aim of being of benefit to the wider society rather than swelling the coffers of industrialists. The fact of the matter is that we produce easily enough wealth in our world to act as responsible stewards of our planet and give every man, woman and child a rewarding and fulfilling life and it only needs someone to allocate it fairly. Almost everyone on this planet can contribute something, and those that can't we'll look after. Once the profit motive is relegated to its rightful ranking we can start to make progress in real terms, social and environmental.

The Law
A problem that will always be with us is criminality, and a most significant part of any society is its police force. It doesn't matter how well thought out and benign a system is it's simply a pipe dream unless it's enforced. There'll always be those who argue under strict philosophical or religious dogma that no one has the right to exercise power over another, and if we allocate one island for any consenting adult anarchist on the planet I'm fine with that. I think though that after thousands of years of social evolution that ship sailed long ago and we need to enforce

civilization in a civilized way. The vast majority of inmates of our prisons are essentially there for the crime of being poor and uneducated, and an enormous problem we have in our current culture is one that's both burdening the penal system and sponsoring inequality worldwide, namely rampant and deliberate tribalism. We're indoctrinated into seeing miscreants who steal cars, smash bus stops, cause gang wars through drug related crimes and other petty criminals as the dregs of society. The fact is that these are desperate, abandoned citizens whose ultimate crime is uncontrolled frustration created by this Frankenstein's monster and are just the latest generation in a long line of generations whose lives and aspirations have been reduced to being cannon fodder for the greed elite.

The prison systems of all nations are stocked with those relegated to who their manipulators have characterised as their tribal nemesis, resigned to existing on the fringes of society, and ultimately the penitentiaries of the world. These stockpiles of wasted humanity are a direct, even contrived consequence of this sick system manufactured from the top down. People must be forcibly educated to the ridiculous fallacy of tribal inferiority which infects every corner of our planet, whether it be ethnic hatred or religious ignorance. A constant on-going program of re-education would involve compulsory involvement in collaborations between ethnic groups and genders in an attempt to discourage and ultimately banish tribal schisms throughout every strata of society.

A monetary system will always allow miscreants to launder and extort their ill-gotten gains, whereas a credit system would involve all finances being held on a database and monitored to protect vulnerable targets of these criminals and highlight duplicitous international launderers. In a Capitalist society this control would be the death knell of entire populations to the greed of their administrators, but a responsible administration could write new constitutions to ensure that responsible stewardship of our wealth meant it was controlled and distributed fairly. There'll always be ways that devious people will devise to side-step the system, a major one for instance is insurance fraud. Something to be considered is that the majority of spurious insurance claims filed by people at the bottom rung of the ladder would radically reduce that temptation once a system propagates fairness and equality in employment and opportunity.

Claims would still be dealt with diligently but there would no longer be individual private companies benefitting or suffering from either premiums or claims and everyone would pay the same rate. Without ownership of insurance by greed driven individuals the responsibility would be on the state for responsible governance without the wickedness of the profit incentive. If you think that this state owned loan of assets is a radical departure then think about it, nothing would be different. We're simply indoctrinated historically by the greed elite establishment to react to phrases like 'state-owned' or 'people's' specifically because it threatens their rule. I well remember years ago when my wife at the time was given a company car and in my ignorance I said "Well that doesn't seem fair, we're paying for it but it's never ours" until I thought about it, it would never be ours! Think about your house or your car, do you own them? All we ever do is lease our possessions from someone else for our entire life, the only difference would be that instead of huge fees extorted from us to make an individual a profit that contribution would be controlled fairly and remain in society for the welfare of the people.

Government
There's an issue to address which, if it hasn't already occurred to you then I'll introduce it. Firstly let's review a few stark facts. Democracy is a farce! If you believe that Democracy is some altruistic tool gifted to setting us free then you simply haven't understood the reality of the world. A society needs to be governed by wise, sympathetic, lenient, impartial benefactors and if you're still under the delusion that western Democracy was introduced to achieve this or could even possibly achieve this then there's really no hope for your comprehension of the realities of human nature. Your pre-programmed response to none 'democratic' alternatives is the delusion that you think you wouldn't have control, well guess what – you never have! Democracy was simply designed by western greed elitists to give that illusion as a smokescreen while they run their dictatorship from the shadows over you. We need a council of elders, not a fantasy council but a real one, to 'govern' a society that can never organise itself in any other way, so that we can move on from this Lord of the Flies system of government. So the issue to address is – who would it consist of? You think you could have individuals put themselves forward and

canvass for election to these posts? Wait a minute we've already tried that. Our society is so riddled with selfists and Tribalists that any candidates would ultimately be sponsored by individual interest groups at each and every level of the 'information' that an electorate would be expected to be made aware of just as it's always done. Governance of societies is too important an issue to be left to a popularity contest amongst people who can never understand the implications of their actions. Democracy is the polar opposite of responsible government unless used in its original limited format so that responsible, lenient members of its panels administer and steer them for the genuine good of all society. Postings to these supreme councils must be accountable and allow for removal, but the appointments themselves have to be 'made' by wise heads not elected by a malleable, gullible, naive electorate. Without the cancer of Tribalism we could dispense with large numbers of departments historically allocated for trade, finance (in an ideal world defence) and foreign affairs, so that we can prioritise things like healthcare, science, engineering, infrastructure and the arts with the naturally reduced administrative positions it would bring. Spending would be equal throughout society without regions vying for a larger share of the budget as the councils would decide where to prioritise funding. Although the advisory panels would comprise of experts in the relevant fields their role would be as support, but the overall direction would need to be a social minded supreme chamber with executive powers for social direction.

Remember that wealth/money is the representation of a society's labour shown as credit and let me give you some information to help you see the full picture of the problem the way it is now, bearing in mind that each citizen is born and exists throughout the entirety of their life in equality in a fair and just society. In the UK in 2016 it was estimated that the richest 1% owned 24% of its wealth. 821,000 households in the UK are millionaires of which 134 are billionaires, and by the end of 2016 the total wealth of British millionaires had also bloomed reaching £6.5 trillion, up from £6.1 trillion a year earlier. In 2017 Britain's wealthiest 1,000 people had a record total wealth of £658 billion mostly from property development for the super rich or investments. The huge levels of inequality in the UK were revealed in a detailed assessment that also showed the richest 5% of people in the country own 44% of its wealth. Did you know that the most supremely privileged individuals aren't even included in financial statistics? All this is without even considering the vast amounts we spend on armaments and other hidden programs that are unaccounted for in official figures. Do you start to see the solution? It's not rocket science. Not only are the greed elite bleeding us for their own wealth and security they're also stripping us of any tiny benefits in public services, social and medical care. The depravity they exercise shows there are no depths to which they won't sink. Other societies have dabbled with a Utopian dream and in every instance they've been targeted by other nations with a vested interest in destroying it, whether it be armed Soviet intervention or discreet American interference, even using their armed forces who've been fooled into thinking they're fighting for 'their' country. Imagine the possibilities of a society that could gain the support and cooperation of their armed forces to allow them to take back their civilization, but would another Stalin hijack it and so allow America to dictate the international agenda with its slow poisoning with the seeds of greed? Think of all the technological advances we've historically squandered under these monsters. It's worth repeating those aspirational sentiments. "We hold these truths to be self-evident: that all men are created equal; that they are endowed by their Creator with certain unalienable rights; that among these are life, liberty, and the pursuit of happiness". Most importantly these evils must never be allowed to happen again and scrupulous monitoring of the press and media in general must be a grave concern at all times.

Practical Action
Each and every one of us of voting age can do something significant towards this Utopia now. We don't need to take to the streets and fight, we don't need to preach for sanity and compassion on a soapbox, we need only to vote for a socialist government. If every country on the planet with a socialist party spontaneously elected them it would be the equivalent of making an ingenious, surprise first move in a game of chess against a grand master. Granted this grand master would react subtly with a deluge of propaganda and possibly aggressively by covert radical sponsorship of right wing oppositions, but we can do it! This would at least usher in an era of openness and tolerance so that we could begin to address the true issues and not be

shepherded through life blinded by a band of selfist manipulators bent on guiding us towards oblivion in order to pamper their elitist self-serving agenda.

8 EPILOGUE

If ever I notice there's a celebrity I've grown up with who's died recently it always make me think of the current events they didn't get to see. Naturally it starts me thinking of the events I'll miss, and the older I get the more I realise that I'm better off out of this hell we're allowing to be created, as the greed elite and their willing acolytes desperately try to convince us that things'll get better and everything's fine, driving this bus towards the cliff and singing as they go. I don't blame anyone for trying to survive as best they can within the structure they were born into, it's human nature after all and the majority of us are just trying to survive. What I can't forgive is those same fortunate beneficiaries perpetuating that unjust system, whether it be the entrepreneur, entertainer or the working class person made good. Throughout modern culture we've experienced fictions positing alien invasion, political subversion and natural disasters, but here we are in the real world literally facing the death of our species, but these mindless greed manipulators are still spreading the seeds of lies to avert the attention of the gullible and naive away from its reality.

Society has developed a cosseted environment where our youth is delicately massaged into their consumer dreamland, completely bypassing that necessary rebellious stage vital to developing new outlooks in social reform. In my youth, and the youth of generations before me, we had our own culture independent of that conservative, ordered world. It was easy to become part of these cultures by adopting the dress code and accoutrements which could be as simple as a pair of bleached or torn jeans or tee shirts which could be easily obtained, and for a fairly affordable sum you could acquire a beat up guitar, bass, drums or even a keyboard. People with a talent for music or poetic expression needed nothing more than these basics in order to provide that much needed vanguard for the up-and-coming generation which was due to inherit the world. We had youth clubs which meant that there was a place for teenagers to congregate where you could mingle and hear songs with the inconspicuous chaperone of a volunteer adult. There was always the public face of the establishment, and if you look at film or TV from the past we can see that underground youth culture has never been accepted into mainstream media until substantially after its original inception, where it would only become broadcast as mainstream once it had been tamed sufficiently. That entire underground culture has gone down a path where bands purporting to be underground are largely avaricious capitalists pretending to be pop stars, and it makes me wary and suspicious of the manipulation of contemporary youth culture. The teenager now seems to be a fleeting phase of post childhood before the materialistic mandarins cultivate them from social media addicts into their commercially driven prison and are then processed through the pseudo science cathedrals before those seeds of rebellion can flower. The underground scene is so sparse it hardly exists at all, instead icons are followed almost exclusively through mainstream media, not because of the message they bring, rather they're an aspirational icon draped in expensive jewellery and clothes, usually in an expensive car with a retinue of women to whom they refer as 'bitches'. It has more of an air of a soft porn commercial than an art contribution. Even the female objects of this vanity parade portray themselves as willing accessories to this hedonistic cult. I'm no prude, far from it, and yes it's acceptable for us to recognise the biological role played through evolutionary urges in the arts, but surely we should aspire to appreciate more than just the soft porn and greed qualities of our species in popular art and culture? Maybe women allow this acceptance as a form of emancipation, where they don't appreciate a deferential hand from any 'gallant gentleman', but unfortunately I see it as just another relegation of respect sacrificed on the altar of avarice. It always perplexed me how women fell for the Capitalist trick of 'Girl Power' as though it was in some way to do with feminism or emancipation, and couldn't see that it was simply a tool of encompassing a wider demographic under their manipulator's profit influence. Niche programmes can pander to a whole variety of interests, but the public image of what we aspire to be as a society should be more than just thinly veiled titillation. Anyone from the past who was told that contemporary songs were now little to do with musical instruments and more to do with the spoken word would be excited. The expectation would be of an enlightened band of poets and rebels, spreading a gospel of freedom or deep consciousness as a counterpoint to the conservative world of their elders. Instead the words are mostly inane repetitive phrases of debauchery or criminality reflecting their despondent view of the world and entice the new breed of greed emerging. Most worrying of all their culture isn't one of rebellion, rather a selfish desire to climb that capitalist pile to the top. The Capitalists have even conquered our youth culture.

If we ever finally emancipate the citizens of the world an assessment has to be made and an inventory of the devastation caused, much in the way that a defeated Germany gave up its dark hidden secrets after the Second World War. It was a time where legions of workers realised through that devastation that the old mindset of 'us and them' was a fallacy and comradeship could create wonderful societies producing advanced socialised medical care systems, equality of the sexes and emancipation of the ordinary citizen as a whole. We have our beautiful blue planet sick and dying with countless species going or already gone, and the ever-diminishing food supplies unable to feed an unnecessarily large population granted their growth so that greed elitists could use them as collateral for their selfist aims. Perhaps in the end we'll never escape and human nature will allow these hunter-gatherer manipulators to finally destroy everything, leaving nothing but the relics of a civilization to be found by a passing traveller and wonder if this is the fate of all civilizations. If we're to win this war then at least we have to stand with those brave enough to suffer these slings and arrows and not be lulled into this greed cult with the distraction of tribalist deceptions. Even if we aren't brave enough to stand on the barricades we can lend our voice to those who are and keep lending it. Even in a perfect world there's so much to put right, but we need to at least start and not let this happen again, being always vigilant. I'm not a student of poetry by any stretch of the imagination, but there's one piece by the American poet Robert Frost called "Stopping by a Wood". Meant as a dedication to the Minutemen who stood ready at a minute's notice to repel their British oppressors it can be interpreted in so many ways and always seems to me an allegory of life itself. I see it as someone who's an emissary on a mission, a small cog in the machine who while pausing briefly, selfishly admires the beauty of the landscape before resuming their duty and continuing with their quest. The last verse goes "For the woods are lovely, dark and deep, but I have promises to keep, and miles to go before I sleep, miles to go before I sleep".

Statistical figures in chapter 7

Coutts & Co Banking
Wealth structuring 22nd August 2017

The Independent Online 22nd November 2016

As a young man growing up in the seventies misogyny and racism was an uncomfortable everyday reality. The advent of The football Premiership promoted idolism of various nationalities and along with black music like Hip-Hop and Rap it promoted black icons of African American culture. I've never been a fan of either genre of music, but the underlying feeling I had was one of a maturing of cultural attitudes to a point where I thought finally we were on the road to true inclusion. With the overnight advent of contemporary British, American and Russian administrations however my faith in human nature has been destroyed and I despair of ever living in a truly fair and inclusive society. I don't honestly know if I could enforce the brutalities necessary to bring about that necessary change, but deep down I honestly feel that there isn't much of an alternative. The people who have the material and power will simply not give it up without being forced, and while they control the organs of disinformation Democracy will continue to be their weapon of choice to keep it.

A better world is possible

* 9 7 8 1 7 9 0 7 1 1 9 9 4 *